EXPLODING YOUR SALES

CONTENTS

INTRODUCTION 3

Introduction to Pricing 4

Starting Your Pricing Strategy 5

The Overall Picture 5

Pricing Considering Competition 7

Rule 1: Only use premium goods Sell for High Prices 8

Rule 2: It's a mistake to be impressed by price 9

Avoid being afraid.. 9

Business Must Adapt to the Changing Times.................................. 10

Boost Sales by Offering Options 11

Benefits for Clients More money in your pocket equals 12

Trials and Lead Gen 12

Getting Rid of the Word Cheap 14

Worth Added.. 15

Summary 17

Added Value Overview 24

What Adding Value Means.. 25

Closing dates 26

Doing Limited Numbers Right 27

Common Testimonials 28

Comments - But Better 28

The Perfect Reference 29

The Basic Bonus 30

Bonuses, But Wiser... 31

Right Bonuses Done... 31

An extra little something 37

Summary 39

DISCLAIMER NOTICE

INTRODUCTION

Let me put a question to you. How did you decide on the pricing you would charge for your own goods the last time you released it for sale online or even offline?

At which we'll be making sales?

My best guess is that you looked at the competitors to see what prices they were charging. While this is a fantastic place to start, it is by no means the complete picture, and if competitiveness is the only consideration you make, you are stumbling in the dark.

You may double your sales volume by increasing your pricing, did you know that? I'll demonstrate how I did it since I did it myself.

Did you realize that 99.9% of the goods I see being marketed are way too affordable? In fact, despite what they undoubtedly believe they are doing, they are turning away clients instead of enticing them.

To ensure that you get the most money in your pocket the next time you launch one of your items, let's dispel some pricing myths and get right to the real facts.

INTRODUCTION TO PRICING

To explain fluid pricing techniques and to demonstrate that there are far more options available to you than at first look.

To address some of your queries regarding how to price your goods for optimal profit while taking into account sales to price ratios.

To demonstrate the negative effects of overpricing, where many people set their prices for their items without first considering the very crucial wider picture.

To demonstrate why many people significantly undervalue their products and how to prevent this mistake.

To demonstrate to you that setting your product's pricing is about more than just charging less than your competitors—setting a higher price can really result in more sales.

To provide you with extra pricing options for your primary product and demonstrate how you can greatly boost your revenues by simply providing your customers choices.

To illustrate the best and most efficient way to introduce trial periods for your items and why many people do this incorrectly.

To demonstrate to you practical strategies for gradually adjusting your pricing without upsetting customers who have previously purchased from you at a higher price.

STARTING YOUR PRICING STRATEGY

Before you go off and make a sales system, launch a website, and slap a price on your product, there are some aspects regarding pricing that I want to discuss with you.

This report's objective is to provide some insight into the range of options you have as an internet marketer using your own goods. The issue is that most individuals tend to simply slap a price on their goods without giving it any thought as to why they chose that price and what elements would determine whether it is a wise choice. Sounds challenging and time-consuming? I'll tell you right now that it's not.

But I think it's crucial that I demonstrate to you how much room there is for experimentation with pricing, as well as the potential consequences of getting it wrong in a variety of ways. As a result, before you announce the price of your product to the public, take some time to read this article, pick up the points, and consider them using them as a checklist.

THE OVERALL PICTURE

Now recognize that there is much more going on here than most people are aware of.

Prices are frequently included for the sake of convenience and may be informally adjusted to account for rivalry and other goods and services that provide comparable benefits, but adding a price tag is not the only goal.

You should keep asking yourself, "Why?" during this procedure.

People occasionally chide me for delving so deeply and discussing the causes of events. They merely want to learn quick and easy ways to make a ton of money.

Well, I tell them, "I can show you how to do things, but if the circumstance changes, and you don't understand why it worked in the first place, then you're going to have to come straight back to me again, pay me another $500 just to figure out how to do the same thing in a different way." If I explain how things work, however, you can gain some significant information and expertise, and you will be more equipped to adjust to the ever evolving world of business, whether it be online or off. You will perish if you cannot adapt. or it is anyway your business.

There's a lot to this, as I said, and there are going to be a lot of topics we'll cover. You're also going to have a lot of questions, of course. Does it matter that there is so much price competition in such a large market?

Do I need to charge less? Should I charge more money? How do I determine which position to take when and why? Should I make specific groups of people special offers?

Who? Why? Should I charge different prices for various product versions?

How do I go about accomplishing it and how can I tell whether I'm doing it correctly?

I'll offer you solutions to all of the questions listed above and many more shortly. However, I want you to be aware of the pricing flexibility you have as an online marketer during this entire process. If you do this correctly, your profits may easily quadruple. If you make a mistake, you can find it difficult to sell anything at all.

PRICING CONSIDERING COMPETITION

After the formalities and generalizations are done, let's look at how to price your products in relation to the competitors. I want to talk about this first for a very straightforward reason. Hey, so what is everyone else charging for similar products? is probably the first thing you'll ask when looking at price. And then you can continue.

There is absolutely nothing wrong with doing this, but there are a lot more factors to consider and inquiries to make than just, "Can I undercut what this guy is charging for his service?"

For you to generate sales, your price should not be lower than the competition's.

I discovered this a long time ago, and you may recall that I talked about increasing sales by raising the monthly membership fee and providing a payment option that was actually 10 times more expensive up front, which further enhanced earnings.

Although it is important to be aware of what competitors are asking for their goods, this does not mean that you must go out and undercut them. Imagine you've just launched a site with an autoresponder script and ad tracking that is so thorough and well-done that it knocks the socks off the competition. However, you can see that the other websites that provide the same service are still operating for roughly $10 per month. Does this imply that you must go out and undercut them in order for people to consider you? Not at all, no.

What you have in your hands is a high-quality item, therefore you shouldn't be concerned about asking a premium for it.

RULE 1: ONLY USE PREMIUM GOODS SELL FOR HIGH PRICES

So this is the first rule. Do not be scared to raise the price if you have a fantastic premium product. To be competitive, you absolutely do not need to undercut your rivals' prices; in fact, it's very feasible that by raising your prices, you will outsell your less expensive rivals. Why? Considering that a higher price shouts quality.

Never think for a second that you must provide the best pricing to close any deals. That is just untrue; if you truly want someone to buy from you again, you simply need to have the best sales system and, of course, a premium product.

RULE 2: IT'S A MISTAKE TO BE IMPRESSED BY PRICE

The truth is that customers will question why you are charging such a small amount if your price is too low. Why does your brand-new piece of cutting-edge software cost only ten bucks if it really is as wonderful as you claim? That concludes rule number two. Never set your pricing so low that you believe consumers would notice and comment, "Wow, that sounds like a decent product, look how cheap it is!" They are not at all stating that. "Wow, look at how little that costs," they exclaim. It can't involve that much.

Therefore, all you are actually doing by raising the price is giving your product even more value. Even though the product might be the same, I'll tell you right now that it's much more likely to sell more copies at a price that makes people think it's fair or average rather than one that makes people gasp in horror at how inexpensive you are.

AVOID BEING AFRAID

Too many people are reluctant to risk it and charge what they think their goods are worth. Too many people, when considering the competition, believe that they must lower their prices or risk losing customers or revenue. Simply said, this is untrue. Don't devalue yourself merely to be less expensive. You charge more for a better product because it is better.

Later on, you can experiment and play around to find the ideal blend of offers, promotions, follow-up, and price alternatives.

I could list a ton of current items that are competing with one another, but one is significantly more expensive than the other. Take this manual, for instance. We're here to charge you $1,000 for the entire collection of instructions, but there are lots of alternative manuals available for just $10. Will both of them be of the same caliber? From the perspective of a customer, I greatly doubt it based just on the pricing.

BUSINESS MUST ADAPT TO THE CHANGING TIMES

How about the most recent item you bought for your home, whether it was a brand-new garage door, a toaster, a dinner table, or anything else? If you give it some thought, I bet you'll realize how much things have changed. People have desired functional items for a very long time—even before I was born. They were only fair. However, that is insufficient today. It must be the best, fastest, nicest, and most straightforward to use. There is a growing demand for high-end goods. If yours is intended to be a premium product rather than a bargain basement item, be sure to avoid putting it in the clearance section.

BOOST SALES BY OFFERING OPTIONS

I'll stop there for now. Another thing that's uncommon, particularly in the area of internet marketing and information products, that I want to discuss is starting off with a variety of price points. People may alter their prices, try out different ranges, make offers, and so on, but if your initial strategy was poorly thought out, none of that will amount to much.

You have choices, even with single-sale information items as straightforward as this one. To be honest, the more the better. Whether you're a high ticket item that offers smaller payments over longer periods of time or a low cost membership site that offers the opposite and charges a single amount for access for three, six, or even a whole year.

Remember that the goal of the sales process is to allay the customer's concerns and dispel any reasons they may have for not purchasing your product. You can't sell someone something and then let them know they can't pay with the method they choose. Make sure to include plenty of these. It's very clear that anyone out there with a website that only accepts one form of payment is losing out on sales. Avoid being this person.

BENEFITS FOR CLIENTS MORE MONEY IN YOUR POCKET EQUALS

The fifth rule is also one of the most crucial. Never, under any circumstances, disregard customers who have already made purchases from you. Finding ways to reward them is not difficult. I'm currently putting together a system for myself that will provide former clients access to a discounted price on my products.

These individuals are the most crucial of all. They are already on your lists, have already made purchases from you, which indicates that they are willing to part with their money, trust you implicitly, and are sincerely interested in learning more about you, your offerings, or both. You'll become bankrupt if you forget this, so keep in mind. That's all there is to it. You want to maintain a positive relationship with the clients who are making purchases from you. If you don't go above and above to win their favor, you'll have to go out and spend a fortune acquiring new clients. Take care of them because they will be a part of your firm for a very long time and will serve as the foundation for its success.

TRIALS AND LEAD GEN

Sixth guideline: Avoid free trials unless you want to generate leads. Free trials have the drawback of drawing all different types of freebie hunters, and just as I don't want anyone here who doesn't want to build a successful business, I'm sure you don't want individuals wasting your time, using up precious resources, and simply choosing anything because it's free.

In order to distinguish between those who are coming to you because they can and those who are serious, it is far preferable to charge a little price for a brief trial, such as one to three dollars for the first week, as I discovered with my large experiment site back in the day.

I also have a fantastic illustration for you here. When we first arrived on the scene, a dear buddy of mine set up a website. He had a fairly solid product that was supported by a matrix-like multi-level affiliate scheme. Anyway, he began marketing, and everything seemed to be going well—that is, until some of his affiliates heard about a site that promised signups but actually sold them for a charge to anyone who would sign up for anything for free.

Now, sadly, I'm sure you can predict what will happen. In addition, the affiliates chose this one, which wasn't much help to them since most of these untargeted people were obviously just freebie seekers signing up because they were getting something in return from the guaranteed signups sites, and only a small percentage were actually going for his hosting package or the pay plan he had in place. What he had in the end was a system jam-packed with customers who had no understanding what they were subscribing to, weren't earning any money for him or themselves or the people who referred them, and had no desire to do so. That was a real resource disaster instance because it practically rendered the pay plan ineffective. Make sure you handle this one correctly and, if your product allows it, provide a trial for a little cost. Otherwise, you can be confronted with a pricey predicament similar to this.

GETTING RID OF THE WORD CHEAP

Rule seven: Don't ever claim that your product is inexpensive. Yuck. Really not much to focus on here, but never ever refer to your things as being inexpensive.

Competitive pricing is good, best price for that service is good, but inexpensive is never a good idea.

Simply said, this lowers the worth of your goods. People rarely seek cheap, in most cases. Particularly in internet commerce, they demand high quality at reasonable prices.

Rule eight: Don't be hesitant to test out different pricing tactics. I can see why you might be concerned that customers who paid $400 for your product could find it inconvenient to receive an email about a special seasonal offer that cuts that cost in half, but it really doesn't work that way.

This won't offend anyone, and it's the only way you can experiment independently and develop new strategies and procedures.

Real world businesses in reality frequently engage in this behavior. They provide huge discounts every day, then raise prices during Christmas and other periods of the year when their products are expected to be in more demand. They also periodically add and remove discounts. It's not wrong to do it. It is not improper. It is work.

Additionally, if your clients have ever ventured outside of their homes to shop, they are aware of this as well.

So here's how it works. Why not give a select group of members a long subscription at a discount of a month or two all year long if you need some additional money? I must say that this one really works, and a big portion of my prior site's member base gave me sizable cash payments up front that I could utilize to further my efforts to increase my income. I might have made a few hundred dollars more over time, but at a slower rate, if I had decided to leave them at their $20 monthly rate.

It's fine if you include discounts at the end of follow-up emails sent after five or six days, and so on. In actuality, there is nothing improper with altering your price on your home page without prior notice. Don't fall into the trap of worrying about what prior clients may think because, on the contrary, this occurs frequently in the actual world. I'm aware that throughout all of my experimental days, nobody has ever confronted me and yelled or complained that I took a quarter off the price the day after they purchased it. It is sufficient to have a high-quality product, and you owe it to yourself to experiment with various approaches, such as those in the aforementioned instances, until you achieve perfection.

WORTH ADDED

9th Rule: Usually add value. We have a full area dedicated to discussing value-adding strategies including bonuses, different strategies, promotions, and the like.

For the time being, just keep in mind that your product shouldn't be the only one while setting a pricing. Indeed, that is a strange statement, but consider it this way: what kind of circumstances will enable you to raise your pricing while also convincing customers to purchase your goods?

The excellence of your product and sales strategy are clear points, but what about bonuses? What about recommendations from reputable authorities in your field?

And it's not just tangible goods. How do people see you and your reputation? So let me leave you with one last piece of wisdom. Use these techniques to raise the value of your goods if you believe it isn't worth the $400 you're asking for it. At this stage, you are aware that you are charging too much for it if you still believe that it is not worth it.

I promise to be open with you now. You must put in some effort if you want to be successful and get your price just right without coming out as "cheap." a little investigation and thought process. It's not all as simple as "one, two, three." Recognize that the key is to price your product appropriately based on the market, the competition, your target market, the product's quality, and the results of your research and tracking. It's not about being more affordable than anyone else.

You ought to know exactly how much you want to charge by this point and how you intend to go about doing it. Excellent if you have. Just keep in mind that the price you list there on launch day doesn't have to be final in any way. It is there for you to fiddle with and experiment with until you feel it is accurate and your testing confirms that it is accurate. Have some self-assurance in your abilities. Try to avoid setting your pricing so low the next time you make a fantastic info product, membership site, or piece of software since, I can guarantee you, doing so will cost you sales rather than bring you any.

SUMMARY

In this section, I'll discuss pricing tactics and demonstrate the range of options available to us as internet marketers when it comes to our own products. Many people appear to just slap a price on their product that they believe it to be worth, or they may look at other prices and try to undercut the competition.

There is more to pricing your goods than first appears because the range and variety of our items and how they are presented is so great.

Many people question why I go into such great depth when discussing costs and other topics. I just want to rapidly make some money, they say, so get on with it. My response to this is that while it's fine if someone explains how something works, you still need to understand the nuances of why something worked in the first place in order to adapt your strategies to changing circumstances without having to purchase a guide every time a new trend emerges. This is especially true in business, where situations change quickly and frequently.

How do we determine our pricing then? What factors should I consider when setting my product's price and does competition matter? Do I need to charge less?

Should I charge more money? How do I determine which position to take when and why? Should I make specific groups of people special offers? And why? Should I charge different prices for various product versions? How do I go about accomplishing it and how can I tell whether I'm doing it correctly? In this section, we'll cover a ton of questions and responses.

Following are my top tips for pricing any product you develop successfully, as well as the questions you should be asking yourself as you proceed, as you should do every time.

Rule number one is to not undervalue oneself. More profit is not necessarily implied by a reduced price.

If I sent you out right now to price up your items, what is the competition charging would probably be the first thought that comes to mind when you're considering pricing? I'll lower my prices.

Remember that your price doesn't have to be the same as, better than, or even near to the prices of your competitors for your products to be successful.

Even if you should be aware of what others are pricing for comparable goods, you don't necessarily have to undercut them. Why is it impossible for your product to compete in your market with Mercedes or Aston Martin? Even though it's an automobile, it's the greatest and a premium item, and the pricing reflects that.

So, the first rule is: Don't be afraid to raise the price if you have a fantastic premium product. You're really more likely to outsell competitors with extremely low prices if you set your pricing higher than theirs. Why? Simple. Would you anticipate the same level of excellence in a $10 course as in a $1,000 course? So that is rule number two. Never set your pricing so low that you assume customers would notice and comment, "Wow, that's a quality sounding product, look how little it costs!"

Since it is not at all what they are saying. They're exclaiming, "Wow, look how inexpensive that is. Which is the catch?

You are essentially just raising the price to reflect the increased value you have added to your product. Even if the product may be the same, I'll tell you right away that it is much more likely to sell at a price that the buyer will find acceptable than at a price that will make the buyer jump out of their chair in disbelief.

Avoid the crowds that are too frightened to even try raising their rates. Don't undersell yourself to be more affordable. You go ahead and charge more for your goods if it is superior. Soon enough, people will learn how valuable you are.

I could list a ton of currently available, competitive items for you, however one is significantly more expensive than the other. Consider using this manual as one. Although we are asking you to pay $1,000 for the complete set of instructions, there are many alternative manuals available for just $10. Will both of them be of same quality? From a customer's perspective, based only on the pricing, I seriously doubt it.

How about your most recent home purchase, be it a toaster, a dining table, an entire work surface, or anything else. The situation was the opposite in the past, if you think back. People desired goods that were reasonably priced, inexpensive, and functional. They were inexpensive and useful. The times have evolved.

It must be the quickest, best, most powerful, loveliest, simplest, and least troublesome to use these days. The greatest moment to benefit from this is right now. If your goods are of a high caliber, avoid placing them in the clearance section. After that, more on this.

Next, provide your clients with options. For instance, a Pro and Lite version. A lite version is excellent because not everyone can afford a premium product.

Additionally, based on the aforementioned justification, provide a selection of expensive products as not everyone can buy them. Selling high-end goods is fine, but as the price increases, you must consider customers who can't make a single purchase, unlike with cheaper goods.

I'll move on to reward programs. Finding methods of rewarding them is simple.

I'm currently creating a system for myself that will provide former clients access to lower prices when they purchase my goods.

The most significant individuals are these ones. They are already on your lists and have purchased your goods, which indicates that they are willing to part with their cash. They also trust you, so you can be sure that they are sincere in their want for additional information about you, your offerings, or both. If you neglect this, you'll run out of money. That's how easy it is. Keep in touch with the clients who are purchasing from you if you want to keep them satisfied. You'll have to spend a ton more money on acquiring new consumers if you don't go out of your way to satisfy them. Take good care of them because they'll be around for a very long time and will serve as the cornerstone of your company's success from the start.

Rule six: Stay away from free trials. Trial periods are frequently a typical component of a membership website, but unless you want to spend your time and money on freebie seekers, set up a brief, cheaper trial for them. For the first month, give customers $1, for instance; otherwise, you might start to question why they aren't purchasing more from you. It's probably because they weren't interested in buying to begin with, which is a waste of your time.

Here, too, I have a fantastic illustration for you. Now, back when we were first starting out, a dear friend of mine built up a website. A multi-level affiliate network, or a sort of matrix, supported his quite good offering. Anyway, he started marketing, and everything seemed to be going well—that is, until some of his affiliates heard about a site that promised signups but really charged money for them, selling signups to anything that was free.

Now, sadly, I'm sure you can predict what will happen. Additionally, the affiliates chose this one, which wasn't much help to them since most of these untargeted people were just freebie seekers signing up because they were receiving something in return from the guaranteed signups sites, and only a very small percentage were actually going for his hosting package or the pay plan he had in place. What he had in the end was a jam-packed system full of subscribers who had no idea what they were signing up for, weren't earning him or themselves or the people who referred them any money, and had no desire to do so. That one was a terrible waste of resources. If your product allows it, make sure to do this one correctly and provide a trial for a nominal charge. If not, you can be facing a pricey situation similar to this.

"Rule number seven." Never claim that your product is cheap. Although it is cost-effective and a good deal, it is never cheap, which implies a lack of quality.

Eighth rule. Experiment with different pricing tactics without hesitation. You might be concerned that customers who paid $400 for your product would be irritated to receive an email for a special seasonal offer slashing that cost in half, and I can see why you might be concerned about that, but it really doesn't work that way. In addition to not offending anyone, doing this is the only method for you to test and develop your own new strategies. Actually, this is something that real-world companies frequently do. They provide huge discounts every day, raise prices during Christmas and other periods of the year when their products are expected to be in more demand, and do a variety of other things. It's just business; it's neither improper nor unethical.

Additionally, your clients will be aware of this if they have ever left their homes to visit a store to make a purchase.

So here's the situation. If you need some extra money, why not give a select group of members a lengthy subscription at a discount of a month or two all year long? I must tell that this one works quite well, and I had a big a percentage of the users from my old site give me big sums of money up front that I could use to expand my revenue. I might have made an additional few hundred dollars, but more slowly, if I had continued to charge them the twenty bucks a month.

Article 9. A substantial portion of our discussion on future value addition, including bonuses, various strategies, promotions, and the like, is included in this section. However, for the time being, keep in mind that your product shouldn't be the only one available when determining a pricing. That is a strange statement, but consider it this way: what kind of factors will enable you to raise your price and genuinely convince customers to purchase your goods?

The excellence of your product and sales strategy are clear points, but what about bonuses? What about recommendations from reputable authorities in your field?

And it's not just tangible goods. How are you perceived by others and what is your reputation? So let me leave you with one last piece of wisdom. Use these techniques to raise the value of your goods if you believe it isn't worth the $400 you're asking for it. Your tracking data will also let you know whether you're charging too much for it at this time if you still don't think it's worthwhile.

Okay, I'll be upfront with you. You must put in some effort if you want to be successful and get your price just right without coming out as "cheap." a little investigation and thought process. It's not all as simple as "one, two, three." Recognize that it's not about offering a product at the lowest possible price; rather, it's about pricing it appropriately based on the market, the competition, your target market, the product's quality, and ongoing tracking and testing.

You ought to be certain of the price you want to charge and the procedure at this point. Excellent if you have. Just keep in mind that the price you list there on launch day doesn't have to be final in any way. It's there for you to fiddle with and experiment with until you think it's perfect. Have some self-assurance in your abilities. The next time you develop that incredible info product, membership site, or piece of software, try to avoid selling it at a loss-leader price because, trust me, you're losing customers instead of gaining them.

ADDED VALUE OVERVIEW

To introduce the ideas of providing value both before and after the sale of your product, keeping your consumers satisfied, and earning more money.

To teach you how to start observing your surroundings and what others, especially successful people, are doing to provide value.

To discuss endorsements and how to use them more effectively so that clients have a strong sense of confidence in you.

To examine regular bonuses carefully and to steer clear of some of the errors that less experienced marketers make when attempting to add value inadvertently and thereby harm their sales.

To provide you three examples of actual marketers who have attempted to add value but failed to do so in one way or another, and to demonstrate how you may avoid seriously harming your sales by doing the same.

To demonstrate how important it is to reward loyalty, consider the fact that doing so can occasionally result in several sales of a single item, which doubles your earnings.

To show how a straightforward strategy may ensure that customers remember you and your goods for a very long time, resulting in future sales and a nice bulge in your wallet.

WHAT ADDING VALUE MEANS

Welcome to the section on improving the value of your items. You might recall that we touched on this briefly in the parts on writing sales letters, but we didn't go as in-depth as I would have liked, so I decided to hold it for this section.

In this section, we'll discuss how to directly affect your sales by enhancing the value of your items through offers, joint venture agreements, consultation fees, bonuses, and other methods. It all comes down to perceived value, you see, and making the most of your goods. Once you've perfected it, you can continually push visitors over the edge to click the buy button on your website. This is something we discussed in pricing strategies: getting the price you believe your product deserves and persuading people to buy it by heaping on reasons for them to do so.

Most importantly, there are many ways to accomplish this and they are constantly evolving as marketers find new and creative ways to enhance the value of their products. In fact, it's interesting observing how they add value to their offer by employing items that aren't specifically relevant to the product itself the next time you find yourself going through a sales letter or some ad material. One of the most essential free methods of doing things you have in your arsenal, watching how others do things on their sites almost entirely eliminates the need for effort, but it works incredibly well. Not just throughout this portion, but always, keep it in mind.

If you're not already working on your product, come back here once it's launched since, with the exception of number two, all of these are components of a sales letter. So let's get going. Why not start at the top, with the most popular and well-known ideas, and work your way down to the newest and most original concepts?

CLOSING DATES

Limitations on dates and quantities: An excellent starting point that is very simple to incorporate into any sales letter for any product. Out of all of these techniques, the traditional cut off dates are perhaps the most popular and continue to be effective. All you need to do is let them know that your reduced pricing is only guaranteed up until a certain date. These are excellent words to employ because they will allow you to extend the deadline without raising any eyebrows. Recently, I've visited websites much too frequently that promise price increases on specific dates, but the price never rises and the date mysteriously advances each day. I can promise you that it is not a good way to conduct business. Although this is more focused on luring impulse shoppers than it is on adding value, I thought it was still important to highlight.

DOING LIMITED NUMBERS RIGHT

The limited numbers approach is next: limiting access to the website to a specific number of users at a specific time or limiting the number of buyers to a specific number at a specific price. Again, a lot of people utilize it, and depending on the strategy, it can both attract impulsive customers and provide value. Now, I particularly like this one. This exact mechanism, where I only allow a few hundred people to sign up at once, is already set up and functioning on one of my prior sites. Naturally, as it is a membership site, I receive recurring money from all of my members, which gives them a sense of serendipity.

Some of them have even admitted as much to me, and I've received inquiries from others on my list wondering when a seat will open up since they were so eager to join.

You might argue that by only allowing a few individuals in at a time, I'm losing money on the trade, but that's not how it actually works. why there is a limit

You might argue this one was discovered by accident because it was originally set up to give me time to begin working on other projects and run my other sites automatically. Remember that if you give it a try—and I urge you to—you can always increase or decrease your limitations. Even if limiting numbers doesn't work for you, doing so at a lesser price almost certainly will. It also never ceases to amaze me how far news of this practice spreads.

COMMON TESTIMONIALS

The quite common and well-liked typical testimonial comes next. Since there isn't much to say and I highly doubt anyone out there has never seen one, I'll just briefly touch on this. A typical paragraph of text that appears throughout your sales letter, along the side of your navigation bar, on a separate website, or in a database of satisfied customers works without a hitch and helps to convince clients that your product is high quality. This is especially true if the author or authors are respected and well-known in your profession. Try to make touch with at least one well-known person, give them your goods gratis, and ask for a review.

COMMENTS - BUT BETTER

Let's now examine the marginally fewer audio testimonials. These further solidify the worth of your goods and vastly boost consumer confidence. I've personally examined text testimonials in the past and discovered numerous obvious problems that convinced me they were fakes. This basically destroyed my first opinion of these items, and I've even had people come to me and admit they've fabricated testimonies in the past. I was obviously unhappy about that. Although it is true that audio testimonies can sometimes be manufactured, this is less likely to come to mind when listening as opposed to reading them, which gives this method a large confidence boost.

It's well worth it if you can collect some audio testimonials, whether you ask folks to leave notes on your answering machine when they phone or you can record over the internet using voice communications. Customers' confidence is greatly boosted by the extra effort, which ultimately leads to more sales and resources for you and your company. not awful at all.

THE PERFECT REFERENCE

Okay, now that we've used both audio and text for these testimonials, let's go all out and use video testimonials with significant bells and whistles professionalism. How frequently do you see live streaming video reviews on websites? I'd say not very frequently. In reality, as of the time of writing, I've only seen two shows in my career, both of which were excellent. Actual people providing real accounts of using effective real products This particular testimonial will be the one that most enhances the worth of your merchandise. A straightforward concept was transformed into a successful, upbeat, hard-hitting approach.

Inviting these people to your home to vouch for the merchandise would be the ideal alternative to video testimonials. I know this is going too far, but with all the digital cameras out there now, the ability to record videos online, and the larger hosting spaces that are starting to surface as a result of the idea competition, getting a couple of them shouldn't take too much time. In my view, it was well worth it. maximization of testimonials.

THE BASIC BONUS

Right, I believe we've covered all we can with those recommendations. Let's move on to bonuses now. standard rewards. Actually, there's nothing fancy about it; all you're doing is providing value by including a bonus with the purchase of the item. These are typically recognized as being closely related to your product or, even better, as being of mutual benefit to both you and the person receiving the free item.

Consider creating a brief training course that customers can distribute so you can gain more credibility and increase the value of the initial sale.

Or, if you're feeling particularly clever that day, how about creating something that will enable you to profit by informing the customer? Give your consumers, for instance, access to an affiliate marketing training that will improve their ability to advertise your products while earning you money.

BONUSES, BUT WISER

Links like these are what make up very brilliant bonuses, even though others who don't grasp your perspective could assume they are just typical. Whether it's more sales, a rebranded book filled with affiliate links or connections to your product they can give away, or an instructional tool that will help your customer and earn you money at the same time, always attempt to create something that will benefit both you and the consumer.

While we're on the subject of using extras to enhance your product, I've actually seen several incredibly successful products that are merely collections of bonuses, with no true core offering. This is something to keep in mind for when you've been running for a while and are having a slow day. Of course, they all have a primary subject and are connected in some way. It is possible to create an entirely new product and source of revenue for yourself if all the items work well together and are relevant.

RIGHT BONUSES DONE

While we're on the issue, would you kindly take notice of this? If you don't, I may have to start questioning people's motivations if I see someone trying to flog their product and believing that an e-book named "Doing Business Today, in the 60's" will help them sell more of it. These kinds of things won't raise your pricing by $500. Let me actually tell you how bad this problem is. If you put together a questionable bonus or go about it the incorrect manner, you risk completely devaluing your product, which will prevent you from selling any. Just like that.

So let me give you a general principle. Go with nothing or build an original info product yourself if you've really thought about it, looked around, and attempted to discover anything to include as a decent valuable extra to try and push clients over the edge and encourage more of them to buy your product. No bonus is preferable to one that turns off all of your consumers. As obvious as it may seem, it seems to be happening more frequently nowadays, which is odd given the overwhelming amount of people who claim to be experts who are instructing people on how to do online business these days.

Using the aforementioned example, I'd like to show you something else that appears to have spread like a strange epidemic and essentially causes me and everyone else I know to leave their website and look elsewhere for their products: when someone spends too much time and effort enhancing one of their products. They at least believe that. How many times have you seen this recently, please? Take a look.

Example: Get your hands on the "Improve Your Fishing" intense training course, which consists of two CDs jam-packed with audio and video and teaches you all the tips, tricks, and techniques that some of the world's top fishermen employ today. . Order today to receive this tested course, which is valued at over $2500, for just $300. In fact, I'm going to lower the price even more because I'm so sure it will benefit you. All of this knowledge is available in one location for an unbelievable $49.95. Order a copy right away!

You get where I'm going, right? Don't get me wrong, there's nothing wrong with catering to impulsive customers, bargain hunters, or just to show folks they're getting a really good deal out of you by offering special deals to those who buy there, but from $2500 down to $49.95? That's going too far and, regrettably, merely makes your product appear to have a flaw. What would you think if a top-of-the-line 85" screen TV was reduced from $3000 to $200 as soon as you walked into a store? You would probably think, "Yeah right, this is a joke," or, more likely, "What's the catch?" or "What's wrong with it?" I can tell you that.

Remember how we discussed boosting client trust in your products? The goal of a sales letter is to eliminate any problems or concerns customers may have with a product while simultaneously generating interest in, and occasionally even a need for, it. Do you see how going overboard or adding too much value too soon could be harmful? While you may view it as offering the clients a deal, they may view it as raising yet another query. Before consumers purchase your product, they must overcome yet another obstacle or resolve a query. Today, it is everywhere. Discounts aren't necessarily a bad thing on their own, but in this situation, they'll kill your sales. Most folks aren't even sure of the reason. If you didn't previously, you do now.

Avoid making the same error.

Now, one thing I don't want to do is make you believe there is only one horrible way to enhance (or completely detract from) the value of your items because I've seen it done countless times in various situations. Originally, I was going to offer you three examples, but let's use the fishing example from above as a starting point. From there, I'll give you two more scenarios, both of which will negatively impact your sales results. Keep in mind that these are actual, current examples that can be seen online.

As an example: Factor "Only want your bonuses" I arrive at this lovely blue and white, expertly constructed, well-designed website, and it makes me grin right away (Just feels nice when something is presented like this). I continue reading the sales material, which briefly explains how I may receive free money-making advice if I subscribe to their newsletter. I see back issues linked here as well, so I'm not turned off by the idea that this is just another lame reason to send me advertisements. The normal "join up today and get this freebie" follows. I'm pleased because it seems to be pertinent to my goals. Normally, at this point, I'd just go ahead and sign up, but this guy chose to go above and above to win my favor.

Software 1, Software 2, Software 3, Software 4,5, Software 6, and so on. E-books 1, E-books 2, E-books 3, E-books 4, and so on. However, are people really signing up for their free email for the freebies or for the content? On the surface, this would seem to be adding value to the point where consumers can't refuse. Again, increasing your subscription count seems positive at first. Actually not at all. Not if they just wanted your collection of 50,000 ebooks and didn't care about your content. Always keep in mind that quality, not quantity, is the most important factor, and this example perfectly illustrates how adding too much value to a free product can ultimately work against you. Your quality suffers, your finances suffer, and your time is completely wasted.

As an example: The "I'm not sure what's happening" aspect Here's an excellent one that I encounter frequently and another that is also becoming more prevalent. Since we sell the instructions that instruct you to market your extras as standalone goods, I genuinely believe that this one is our fault. Although this information is accurate, it can be misused.

I'm browsing the internet once more when I stumble across a site that happens to be a money-making scheme. Of course, I have nothing against money-making chances, and this one just so happens to have a catchy headline that makes me want to read more. The sales message becomes better as I read further down until we reach the goodies. Ebook 1, this e-book (which directs me to a brand-new sales letter), this software (which directs me to a brand-new sales letter), and so on for three or four bonuses. By the time I'm done, I've read six sales letters that each attempt to pitch me on to something else, have five windows open, and am having problems navigating back to your sales letter.

It's crucial to keep in mind to use incentives to provide value in a way that makes them look like actual products, but never ever lose sight of what you want your website to accomplish. Don't make consumers read ten sales letters for various products in order to confuse them. It simply doesn't operate that way. Once more, despite your belief that you are giving value, all you are really doing is confusing and diverting your visitors. When someone says, "Sell your bonuses like a real product," they mean, "Sell your bonuses like a real product." They mean, "Sell your bonuses like a real product." They mean, "Sell your bonuses like a real product." Don't overdo it or you'll lose clients once more.

Just the two aforementioned examples (three if you count the fishing one) are what I see on a daily basis, and the worst part is that when people ask me, "Why aren't there any sales from my site?" and I respond that certain elements of their bonuses sections are killing their sales letter, they give me strange looks and comments. I can tell they don't feel particularly proud about that, but it's like one of those tiny bothersome mind games where the answer is so clear that people miss it. No issue at all; as long as you learn from it and don't make the same mistake twice, I assure them, you'll be OK.

Don't worry if you've read this far and are still unsure of what in the world you could provide as a bonus in addition to your goods or if you don't have any extras on hand. It's not even necessary for it to be physical. It doesn't have to be a piece of software or an outdated electronic book— in fact, that would probably be advantageous. Consider alternative things you could provide to consumers in addition to your offering, and try to be a little more flexible. Are you well-liked in your line of work? What if you offered your customer a free, no-obligation one-hour phone or video session along with their purchase? You could even offer them a follow-up appointment to find out how they are doing with the product you just sold them.

If you have the information, putting this into practice isn't all that difficult. Personally, I value my downtime, so you won't get me on the phone to discuss your company unless you've just deposited $500 into my account for the hour. Heck, you'd have to get to know me fairly well and be on good terms with me to get me down to that amount either. The fact that it took a bit longer than three hours to prepare this guide immediately adds value to the product without my even having to give advice. You can do this as well, and if you really wanted to go above and beyond, there's nothing wrong with giving away free consultations for up to an hour per customer, depending on how many clients you expect to have each week. Don't try to offer a free three-hour session to 100 people every week.

To bring any of this together, you don't need to be in the business of selling manuals and business information. No matter what you're offering, you can employ this technique anywhere, whether it's an hour of free technical support or a complimentary 30-minute confidence booster. You are entirely in charge.

Be creative, and who knows? It might even result in more consultations, which would put more money in your pocket. A free gift benefits you as well as your consumers, not just them. A significant factor that you should consider when producing any kind of value-adding content. How does this benefit both me and my clients?

AN EXTRA LITTLE SOMETHING

There are two additional approaches to add value to a product that I'd want to discuss with you before we move on. But this time, unlike most extras, the bonuses we'll be giving away have nothing to do with the product and won't necessarily be mentioned in the sales letter. Giving the client a little extra is always pleasant, and this is one way to do it while once again, as we've said, benefiting both you and the consumer.

The first instance I'd want to discuss is introducing a ticket system that allows you to offer discounts on your other products, either now or in the future. Allowing customers to add more items to their shopping cart at a discounted price and then check out is an excellent approach to accomplish this. They can get something additional for a little less, and you can generate more sales at the same time, which is advantageous to both you and your customer.

It doesn't hurt to provide loyalty discounts if this is your first product. Consider offering them 10% off your company's next product that they purchase. On the surface, it might not seem like it will make a big difference, but if you can turn a one-time buyer into a loyal customer who keeps coming back to you time and time again, that is the best way to add value to your products because it will benefit you in the long run when past customers start buying multiples of your goods within a year.

The last thing is about rewarding loyalty, which is something that is underappreciated and seldom ever used (at least based on the products I've bought over the years). If you decide against include specific bonuses on the sales letter for some reason, why not try something a little different and surprise the customer with it after they purchase the product? Granted, by not including this in your sales letter and giving it to customers after the sale, you are losing out on some potential sales, but I assure you that if you do this, you will be remembered and, more importantly, people will talk about you and, as a result, become lifelong, devoted clients of yours. Is there anything of greater worth?

Above all, if you recall nothing else from this, I want you to keep in mind that no business decision is final. Nothing that works now will continue to work in the future, and neither do current regulations.

Everything that has been written before you also holds true. Try new things, stand out from the crowd, and you'll be remembered. You'll also make tons of money and establish a name for yourself. Who knows, in six months you might be sitting where I am right now, typing a report outlining the newest and most innovative marketing strategies you've learned on your journey.

SUMMARY

In this section, we'll explore how to increase sales by directly influencing the concept of adding value. This will include using carefully crafted offers, joint venture agreements, consultations, bonuses, and other strategies to show that the perceived value of intangible goods is equivalent to the monetary value of tangible goods.

There are numerous ways to increase the value of your product, and there are always fresh and creative ways to use tried-and-true tactics. The next time you read a persuasive sales letter from a reputable marketer, pay attention to these and consider how they are enhancing their offerings. One of the most valuable free and nearly effortless methods of study you have at your disposal is to observe how others conduct themselves on their websites, and it works incredibly well. Not just throughout this portion, but always, keep it in mind.

Cutoff dates and limited quantities for your sales letters are an excellent place to start in this situation. The one that gets the sales flowing the most if done properly, aside from testimonials, is probably the most common and well-known.

The only thing that cut off dates call for is a warning that a special deal is ending on a specific day, creating the sense that the reader will miss out if they don't buy now, an old-fashioned and frequently employed but successful strategy for driving up sales.

If you opt to use this strategy, be sure to include language stating that your reduced pricing and special offer are only valid until a specific date. By doing this, you may avoid employing those tiny java codes that advance the date by one day each day in relation to the visitor's computer clock time.

Second, consider limiting access to your website to a specific amount of visitors at a given time. Again, this is extremely common and both encourages impulsive purchases and adds value. This method is in place on one of my old sites, and even now, I get inquiries from people wondering if a spot has opened up and even making higher offers than the usual entry cost.

You might argue that by only allowing a few individuals in at a time, I'm losing money on the trade, but that's not how it actually works. You might argue I found this one by mistake because the limit was initially set so that I would have time to begin working on other projects and could operate my other sites on autopilot. Remember that if you give it a try—and I highly encourage that you do—you can always increase or decrease your limitations. Even if limiting numbers doesn't work for you, restricting numbers at a lesser price almost certainly will.

The testimonial is the next strategy for increasing value. Even though we've already discussed this, it bears repeating. A normal paragraph on your sales letter, down the side of your navigation bar, or perhaps an entire section devoted to client feedback and testimonials. This is quite effective at adding value to your items and proving their capabilities.

Developing testimonials further: Consider adding sounds. A simple way to add authenticity and a little bit of plausibility to your customers' comments is to simply set up your answering machine to record and inform your customers that they can leave audio testimonials there. Additionally, since audio testimonials are difficult to fake, you're building even more reader trust.

Why not go one step further and include video testimonials? This was done by a particular marketer I observed a few months ago, and it gave his sales letter a lot of stickiness, memory, and strength. If you have the means to put one together, I strongly advise you to do so because I tend to forget about sales letters within a few hours unless I learn something new or they are exceptionally special and one-of-a-kind.

Standard bonuses will follow. Again, since we've previously covered the fundamentals, let's move on. Instead, how about going a little bit further with traditional additional giveaways?

What if you created a little training course that the client could distribute for free, enhancing the value of the initial sale while also helping you establish your reputation?

Or, if you're feeling really clever that day, why not create something that will enable you to profit by informing the customer. Giving out an affiliate marketing training to your consumers will help them grow as affiliates, which will hopefully help them advertise your products and earn you money at the same time.

Links like these are what make up genuinely brilliant extras, even though they may appear ordinary to those who don't understand your perspective on the surface. Always attempt to create something that will be advantageous to both you and the consumer, whether it be more sales, a rebranded product packed with affiliate links or links to your product they can give away, or an instructional tool that will help your customer while also generating revenue for you.

While we're on the subject of offering bonuses to bolster your product, I've actually seen some incredibly successful goods that are merely made up of a plethora of freebies, with no real focal point of focus. They all have a unifying theme and are connected in some manner, of course, but this is something to keep in mind for when you've been running for a while and are having a slow day or want to put together a feature-rich membership site. When all the items work well together and are pertinent, you can create a completely new product and source of income for yourself.

The following is my main point: Don't diminish value by adding to it. Imagine if I attempted to give you a bonus with this course, referred to it as "Business in the modern 1960s," and then proceeded to tell you it was worth $500, perhaps as an antique, but nothing more.

Go with nothing if you've truly considered it, looked around, and attempted to find something to include as a worthy extra to try and nudge clients over the edge and encourage more of them to buy your goods but you can't find anything that meets the criteria. A bonus that turns off all of your consumers is preferable to none at all. Even though it is so obvious, it seems to be happening more frequently nowadays, which is remarkable given the vast amount of experts who are now instructing individuals on how to run their own internet businesses.

Your price comes next. Have you ever seen things that claim to be worth $500, then next to it have a new price crossed out with the old $250 price checked out, then that price is crossed out, and finally next to it have a $20 price tag? I believe that individuals are smarter than a lot of sales letters suggest.

It's okay to send these kinds of signals to individuals, but from $500 to $20? Not in my opinion. Yeah, that's right, this is a joke, or more frequently, what's the catch? or "OK, what's wrong with it?" is the response. just undervaluing to the point where clients get doubtful once more

See how going overboard or adding too much value too quickly can be harmful? They perceive it as a new query, whereas you see it as offering the customer a deal. Yet another obstacle they must overcome or a query they must resolve before purchasing your offering. These days, it's commonplace. Discounts are not terrible in and of itself, but in this situation, they will destroy your sales. A lot of folks don't even understand why.

In if you didn't previously, you do now. Don't commit the same error.

Here are three instances of people who gave up too much value to their harm in real life that I witnessed. First, I arrive at this elegant website that has been carefully designed in blue and white, which makes me grin right away. I continue reading the sales text and am happy to say that it makes the free publication sound quite alluring. I'm prepared to join up, but this person decides to make an extra effort to attract me before I do.

E-book incentive In addition to a collection of forty electronic books, there are also programs 1, 2, 3, 4, 5, 6, 7, 8, 9, and 10. I had forgotten the name of the original product by the time I had finished reading about each one. On the surface, it could appear to provide value, but are individuals really joining up for the bonuses or their free newsletter?

Giving the world away is a fantastic approach to obtain quantity rather than quality.

The second example is an excellent one that I frequently encounter and that you have probably also encountered. In fact, I really believe that we are to blame for this one as we are the ones who are peddling the manuals that advise you to market your incentives as standalone products. Although this information is accurate, it can be misused.

I'm browsing the internet once more when I stumble across a site that happens to be a money-making scheme. Of course, I have nothing against money-making chances, and this one just so happens to have a catchy headline that makes me want to read more. The sales message becomes better as I read further down until we reach the goodies. E-book 1, this e-information book's can be found by clicking here (which takes me to a brand-new sales letter), this software's information can be found by clicking here (which brings me to a brand-new sales letter), and so on for three or four bonuses. By the time I'm done, I have five windows open, been taken all over the place, and am having problems navigating back to the first sales letter.

It's crucial to keep in mind to use incentives to provide value in a way that makes them look like actual products, but never ever lose sight of what you want your website to accomplish. Don't make consumers read ten sales letters for various products in order to confuse them.

There are two additional approaches to improve: The first is offering discounts for additional items at the checkout. Add this to your cart, purchase them all at once, and save 50%. In many circumstances, this is a great and quick approach to generate double sales. More money for you, more worth for the client. Even while not everyone will accept your offer, the few extra sales add up.

It doesn't hurt to provide loyalty discounts if this is your first product. Consider offering them 10% off your company's next product that they purchase. On the surface, it might not seem like this will accomplish much, but when you turn a one-time buyer into a loyal customer who keeps making repeat purchases from you, this is the best way to add value to your items because it benefits you in the long run.

The last thing is about rewarding loyalty, which is something that is underappreciated and seldom ever used (at least in the things I've bought over the years). Why not do something a little different and surprise them with it after they purchase the product, if for some reason you don't want to put specific incentives on the sales letter? Granted, by not including this in your sales letter and giving it to customers after the sale, you are losing out on some potential sales, but I assure you that if you do this, you will be remembered and, more importantly, people will talk about you and, as a result, become lifelong, devoted clients of yours. Excellent value.

Above all things, if you recall nothing else from this portion of the guide, keep in mind that nothing in business is fixed in stone. Nothing that works now will continue to work forever, and neither do any regulations that are in place now.

Everything that has come before you has the same application. Who knows, in six months you might be sitting where I am now, putting out a report like this outlining the most recent marketing techniques that you've discovered. Experiment, innovate, and be distinctive and you will be known, make tons of money, and get your name around.